Introversion in the Classroom

How to Prevent Burnout and Encourage Success

Jessica Honard, M.Ed

ISBN: 152388133X
ISBN-13: 978-1523881338

DEDICATION

For Taormina Lepore, who is a constant source of encouragement, inspiration, and support.

For Marie Parks, who takes all of my new ideas in stride and is always willing to help.

For my parents, who will make sure at least one copy of this book is purchased.

Finally, for all of the educators who spend each and every day giving their all.

Thank you.

TABLE OF CONTENTS

INTRODUCTION

Hello. My name is Jessi, and I am an introvert.

Sometimes, when I am in the company of others like myself, introversion becomes a uniting force. Together, we can puzzle over the mysterious and sometimes overwhelmingly extraverted world to which we are told we must adapt.

Other times, it feels like a dirty little secret.

Like many others, I have spent my life dodging phone calls, hiding in bathrooms and burying my nose in books. I have armored myself against accusations of shyness, social anxiety, and standoffishness. I have obsessed anxiously over presentations, class participation, and the prospect of expressing myself to my peers. I have found myself enjoying social time, only to collapse in exhaustion afterwards, taking days or even weeks to recover from overstimulation.

I am a token introvert, and mine is a familiar story for many.

For years I wondered what it was that made me feel so out of sync with my peers. I didn't have the language to explain what made me different, and I wasn't armed with the knowledge that more people than I realized felt the exact same way.

When Susan Cain's now famous TED Talk about introversion was released in 2012 I was stunned by how relevant it was to my life. Finally, someone who not only understood me, but could tell me exactly why social interaction exhausted me so much.

Cain's talk, and her bestselling book *Quiet: The Power of Introverts in a World That Can't Stop Talking*, opened a new world to me. It showed me that I wasn't odd or awkward, and taught me that I could carve out a comfortable place among the extraverts of the world.

As I absorbed all of this new information, I realized how much better off I would have been in school — both as a student and as a teacher — if I had known about my own introverted nature, and how to adapt my classroom for introverts like me.

I remember all too well how it felt to slouch in my desk, terrified that the teacher would call on me. I also remember the pressure, as a teacher, to incorporate as much collaborative group work as possible into my own classroom.

As educators, we need to commit to a classroom of understanding and acceptance, where students are allowed to learn how to step outside of their comfort zone without being forced to live there. We need to understand and appreciate our own comfort zones, too.

My hope is that through this book you will find the inspiration to design a classroom that elevates extraverts and introverts alike, giving both ends of the spectrum the opportunity to reach their full potential. In addition, you'll find self-care tips for the introverted teacher.

A quick disclaimer: Most of the information in this book is based on a collection of anecdotal findings combined with reading various journal articles. I'm not a trained personality theorist, and I don't have a degree in psychology.

What I do have is a passion for understanding how energy influences the classroom, and how we can create the best learning environment possible. If you find yourself wanting to know more about the research behind personality theory, take a look at the references at the end of this book.

If you're interested in joining the discussion and adding your own experiences and solutions to the conversation, I encourage you to join us. *The Adaptive Introvert* is a community dedicated to keeping the conversation alive. Please join our Facebook group by requesting an invite from our webpage at *adaptiveintrovert.com/join-the-community*. I look forward to welcoming you!

Best,

Jessi Honard, M.Ed

PART I: THE INFLUENCE OF TEMPERAMENT IN EDUCATION

"Everyone shines, given the right lighting." – Susan Cain

DEFINING INTROVERSION

Understanding the Energy Currency

Where does your energy come from? What exhausts you? What uplifts and excites you?

Your answers to these questions are more than a simple matter of personal preference. They have deep implications about how you respond to the world.

If we think of energy as currency, introversion and extraversion represent two very different ways of spending.

Introverts are likely to spend a lot of energy in situations that are highly stimulating. Even if they enjoy it, the introverted student will need to step away and recharge long before the extraverted student. These introverts refill their energy banks by spending time in environments that are peaceful, either alone, or with one or two close friends.

Extraverts crave highly stimulating environments, and as such it takes longer for their energy levels to run low. This doesn't just manifest itself with social interaction. Stimulation can come in many forms, from uplifting music to daredevil adventures. Your extraverts will likely still be in the thick of it long after your introverts have burnt out.

And, of course, there are people who fall in the middle. These **ambiverts** can encounter the benefits and the challenges of both temperaments.

The Introversion-Extraversion Spectrum

Like most aspects of personality, introversion and extraversion do not exist in black and white. Instead, they live at opposite ends of a spectrum, and individuals can fall anywhere on this sliding scale.

Because of this, some introverts will find that they burn out more slowly than others. Some people may even discover that they fall smack in the middle of the spectrum, displaying equal amounts of introverted and extraverted qualities.

Self-identification

Many people have an inherent sense of where they fall on this spectrum, particularly if they are firmly on one end or the other. Below are a few qualities you may find on either side of the spectrum.

The Introvert
1. Tends to be an inward thinker
2. Prefers to work alone or with one or two people
3. Burns out quickly at large parties
4. Prefers to schedule activities in advance
5. Does not always speak up
6. Has a small community of close friends

The Extravert
1. Is quicker to say what is on his or her mind
2. Enjoys frequently collaborative environments
3. Thrives at high energy social events
4. Tends to be more spontaneous
5. May speak up and participate more often
6. Tends to have many friends and make new ones easily
7. Becomes bored or restless when alone for too long

Keep in mind that these are generalizations. There are items on this chart that may not apply to you or your students, despite their temperament. Everyone is unique.

If you're interested in a more thorough test of your introverted qualities, there are quite a few options online.

My personal favorite test is a complete Myers-Briggs Type Indicator®. This series of questions, developed in response to psychological theories by Carl Jung, measures four different aspects of personality:

1) Where you get your energy from (are you **introverted** or **extraverted**?).

2) What information you pay attention to (are you **sensing** or **intuiting**?).

3)   How you process information and make decisions (are you **thinking** or **feeling**?).

4)   How you organize your life and respond to its many demands (are you **judging** or **perceiving**?).

The MBTI® has endured some scrutiny over the years, as have Jung's theories, but it remains one of the most frequently utilized personality tests, and it has the potential to tell you a lot about yourself. It is designed to help you understand how you perceive the world around you, react to it, and organize it. The first of the four measurements the MBTI® takes is a measure of your energy currency. Are you introverted or extraverted — or somewhere in the middle?

Simplified versions of the MBTI®, which may serve as useful gauges within the classroom, are available online. There are also more comprehensive, paid versions (including the official one).

My favorite of the free options is offered on *16Personalities.com*. Not only is the survey thorough, but the explanation offered upon completion is also incredibly detailed. If you're uncertain about your temperament, I highly recommend it.

Understanding Your Opposite

Understanding the dynamic spectrum of introversion and extraversion can have powerful implications for everything, from the success of your students to your own personal health and sense of well-being.

Whether you are an introvert or an extravert, you likely have friends, family members, or colleagues that are your opposite. It's entirely possible that these people do things that completely baffle you.

An understanding of introversion and extraversion may provide some insight to these seemingly strange behaviors. They simply may have different needs when it comes to recharging. Understanding how your opposite performs best will help you differentiate for them.

Extravert or Extrovert?

You may have seen it written both ways. This isn't because people don't know how to spell – both have become commonly accepted as correct iterations of the word.

From a linguistic standpoint extravert is correct. The word "extra" is Latin for "outside", which makes a lot of sense given that extraverts are more focused on their outer, external world.

The spelling extrovert has gained popularity, and is likely the version you'll run across most often. The reason for this may in part be due to the fact that it simply looks better when placed next to the word "introvert". By exchanging the "a" for an "o" the words appear more parallel.

The Extraverted Norm

As a society, outgoing, gregarious personality types are often championed. Individuals are constantly encouraged to be go-getters, to network, and to attend social events that will broaden their contact base. There are countless seminars and classes designed to teach people how to be more outgoing and energetic in public.

None of this is bad in and of itself. Much of it is completely natural for introverts and extraverts alike. Unfortunately, this over-emphasis on outward socialization has created a situation where only a single set of needs are being addressed. By putting forth extraverted traits as the ideal, introverts are inadvertently receiving the message that when they need to seek out alone time to recharge they are doing something wrong.

It is not uncommon for introverts to self-identify as awkward, socially stunted, or shy. In reality, they may be none of these things. They are simply reacting to the exhaustion they feel from the constant pressure to put themselves out there.

This is a message that introverts begin receiving from a very early age, which is why it is crucial for us, as educators, to understand the preferred energy currency of ourselves and our students.

Introvert Myths and Preconceptions

The sense of wrongness that exists around introversion is perpetrated in part by a slew of myths. These negative preconceptions have risen out of a general misunderstanding of what introversion is and how it manifests itself.

Many of these myths are borne from the fact that introverts need to recharge much quicker than their extraverted peers. This sudden need for alone time can be misconstrued in a variety of ways.

Introverts are rude

It's easy for silence to be seen as stand-offishness. If someone is slow to smile they can be considered unfriendly. When someone doesn't engage in small talk, they may be viewed as judgmental.

The fact of the matter is that introverts aren't necessarily looking to engage in conversation, especially if their energy reserves are low. Unless the topic is something they care passionately about, the conversation may cost them too much energy to be worth it. As a result, they will give short, to-the-point answers. This isn't borne out of rudeness. It is simple energy conservation.

Introverts are brainiacs

Intelligence and personality are two separate domains. One may influence the other, but one does not determine the other. It's important to remember that there are many different kinds of intelligence.

Everyone learns a little differently, and an individual's learning style and abilities are not necessarily tied to whether they are introverts or extraverts.

Introverts cannot compete in the workforce (or in the classroom)

Contrary to the previous myth, it sometimes may appear as though introverts are always a step behind their extraverted peers.

Slower to talk, more reluctant to throw out ideas that aren't well thought through, and generally more cautious, it can be easy to worry that introverts are simply falling behind.

Fortunately, this isn't necessarily true. Introverts may approach a problem differently, but their thoughtful, level-headed approach often lends itself to practical solutions.

Introverts do not like people

Despite the fact that introverts sometimes need a break from their stimulating environments, many actually do enjoy company. Remember, they just become over-stimulated more quickly. As a result, rather than finding enjoyment in large groups of people, introverts may prefer to deepen a few select friendships. Your introverted student is much more likely to have a core group of two or three friends than a large social circle.

Introverts are shy

Similar to the second myth, shyness does not necessarily have anything to do with introversion or extraversion. "Shy" refers to a social inhibition, or fear, that prevents active engagement with others, particularly strangers. There are shy extraverts and there are outgoing introverts.

While some introverts may suffer from social anxiety and shyness, this is not necessarily so. Being introverted simply means that excessive socialization (or exposure to bright lights, noise, etc.) is exhausting.

Being introverted is wrong

While I have yet to cross paths with anyone directly promoting the idea that being introverted is wrong, this is a pervasive, subliminal message that introverts are all too familiar with.

Introverts are often being redirected in a manner that makes them feel as though they are behaving in a socially awkward, standoffish, or unacceptable way.

Introverts have their own unique perspective on the world, one that works in balance with extraversion. The extravert is as important as the introvert, and in fact each one balances the other.

Unfortunately, introverts receive this unintentional message of wrongness from a young age, and often with the best intentions. They learn to emulate what is expected of them rather than what comes naturally.

INTROVERSION IN EDUCATION

The modern public school building is a noisy, busy place. It is the very picture of a stimulating environment.

Some of this is sheer necessity. A school is responsible for maintaining order while shepherding large numbers of students throughout the building.

Teachers must manage classrooms that often swell to 35 or more students. Despite the value of individualized attention, there is often little time for it. Teachers are overwhelmed, juggling the mesh of personalities within their classroom while trying to teach the content in a way that is accessible and meets constantly changing expectations.

These crushing responsibilities, faced by school and teacher alike, have led to coping mechanisms that, unfortunately, leave introverted students adrift.

Developing a Sense of Unity

Faced with the monumental task of educating hundreds, if not thousands, of students, the modern public school often focuses on developing a common sense of identity.

Through assemblies, sporting events, talent shows, and other activities schools instill a sense of spirit in the students and staff. As a result, students and teachers take pride in their school and are more likely to be active participants, not just in the educational components, but in its overall culture.

Unfortunately, assemblies and rallies can be an introvert's worst nightmare. Gathering students *en masse* to scream and shout and dance is enough to make any introvert's hackles raise.

These events are also often compulsory. When I was in the classroom students were given two options: Attend the noisy, crowded pep rally, or go to detention.

A surprising number of students chose detention.

The Open Classroom

Once, a well-structured classroom was one where its students sat silently in perfectly aligned rows, listening to the teacher lecture, speaking only when spoken to.

Then, a revolution happened.

The old teaching methods were thrown out, and in its place teachers were taught to embrace the messy, noisy realities of the collaborative classroom. Rows turned into groups, silence shifted into group discussions, and the teacher went from being the center of attention to the facilitator.

Group work, jigsaw activities, discussion and debate – all of these appear frequently as methods that will help students prepare for the world beyond school. Open classrooms that operate in teams or pods have become more and more common. Emphasis is placed on group productivity, and purposeful socialization is encouraged and used to foster creativity and the sharing of ideas.

All of these factors are well-suited to an extraverted student. For someone who thrives on collaboration and high-energy activities, it is the perfect environment. Not only that, but it adequately prepares students for what will be expected in the working world, where extraversion is championed.

There is no denying that teamwork, leadership, and negotiation are all essential skills, and group work is an excellent way for students to learn them.

There is a subtle, but powerful message being delivered in these classrooms.

To be successful, you must be social.

Profile of an Introverted Student

Given what you now know about introverts, it's probably not a surprise to discover that your classroom is likely full of them. As a whole, introverts make up about a third to half of the population. This means that one in every two to three students in your classroom may be introverted.

What does this mean for you, the teacher?

Marti Olsen Laney, the author of The Hidden Gifts of the Introverted Child, notes that children's temperaments – where they fall on the introversion-extraversion scale – impacts the way in which they learn (2005).

Your introverted students are those whose energy stores are depleted by too much time engaging in group work, rushing through loud hallways, and navigating busy lunch rooms. They're much more likely to go home at the end of the day and collapse on their bed than their extraverted friends.

So what are the impacts on their ability to learn when they are constantly being thrown into stimulating situations?

A Cycle of Burnout
Socializing and working well within a team are valuable skills for everyone to learn. There is no denying this.

However, constant stimulation can become incredibly expensive for the introvert. It costs introverted students valuable energy, and when they aren't given a chance to recover, they run the risk of burnout.

In many schools, students are immersed in a highly stimulating environment every day for nine months straight. On top of the usual expectations there are also clubs, athletics, assemblies, and recess. The norm is loud, bright, and full of people.

When burnout strikes, introverted students have little choice but to push it aside and carry on, over-drafting their energy accounts.

An overdraft may manifest itself in different ways, depending on the person and the amount of energy that is being used up. Some possible effects of overstimulation are:

Fatigue

Exhaustion and burnout go hand-in-hand. Depleted of energy, an introverted student may enter a state of seemingly constant fatigue.

It is shocking how quickly this can happen in a school setting, where introverts are overwhelmed by the constant socialization with peers, expectations of teachers, and general cacophony. Add in crowded cafeterias and rambunctious playgrounds, and it's no wonder the introverts of the world want to hide when they return home.

Headaches

An introverted student who is exposed to external stimuli constantly can become overwhelmed and stressed out. One common side effect of stress is the development of headaches. According to WebMD, stress headaches, also known as tension headaches, can last anywhere from minutes to days.

Irritability

If a student is put in a situation where she is forced to continue socializing, even after her energy levels are depleted, it may result in irritability. Students could become frustrated or annoyed with their peers or authority figures, snapping at them or withdrawing into themselves. In some situations, they may even become combative. This in turn only fuels the myth that introverts are rude and dislike people.

Lack of Motivation or Interest

Full-on introvert burnout can make even the most loved tasks seem tedious and undesirable. Your most motivated student stops turning work in on time, or completed. The student who always has a joke on hand fails to deliver. Another student, always eager to dive into a new book, starts to show no interest.

Unfortunately, burnout is everywhere. It is not limited to any particular age group, grade, or ability level. From the earliest ages, students are encouraged to play together, learning in groups. This means that introverts are also put at risk of burning out even when they are very young.

The Introvert in Hiding

Jorge is a Kindergarten student who shows a lot of promise academically. He excels at class work, and has shown quite a bit of creativity. However, during structured play he often becomes withdrawn, refusing to work with the group.

As the school year continues, Jorge shows little interest in group activities. He will occasionally play with one or two of his classmates, but typically prefers to spend his time alone, drawing.

The teacher takes note of this, and tries to encourage Jorge to play with his classmates occasionally. He resists, and she doesn't push him. However, she does bring it up at parent-teacher conferences, telling Jorge's mother that she is concerned he may not be developing socially.

Jorge's mother, also concerned, begins to encourage her son to play outside more. She sets up play-dates, enrolls him in sports and other activities, and encourages him to be "less antisocial".

Over time, Jorge begins to interact with his peers more. He abandons his drawings in favor of group games. At the next parent-teacher conference, Jorge's teacher happily reports that he is progressing well.

If you pulled out your class roster right now and went down the list, odds are that you could sort most of them as either introverts or extraverts.

There's also a good chance that your initial guess is wrong for a number of your students.

Why?

Because not all of your introverts are easy to spot. Many of them are in hiding.

In fact, they may not even know that they are introverts.

As a kindergarten student, Jorge was perfectly content sitting alone and drawing, but his mother and teacher redirected him into social situations so often that he began to do it automatically.

Now imagine Jorge as a junior or a senior in high school. By this time the act of being social, even when it is tiring, has become so second-nature that he doesn't give it a second thought. He doesn't understand why he's so exhausted at the end of every day, and doesn't pursue alone time as a way to recover.

Other introverts may actively hide their more reserved nature. One theorist, Arnold Henjum of the University of Minnesota, notes that, "[w]ith society's tendency to reward those who are socially involved, it is natural that introverts would hide their true feelings regarding how they would like to spend their time" (1982).

The open introverts of the world may face certain stigmas. They often must defend themselves against labels like "quiet," "bookish," "weird," or "nerdy."

Your most outgoing student may be simply covering up his or her exhaustion, forcing themselves to appear more extraverted than they are. They want to be seen as normal, and they have been receiving the message that extraversion is normal for a long time.

FINAL THOUGHTS

Our understanding of introversion and extraversion can have a profound impact on how we relate to others.

In the past few decades, classroom pedagogy has jumped from one extreme to the other. While silent, attentive rows are by no means the most effective way to teach, the new trends are forcing your introverted students to spend massive amounts of energy.

In fact, the entire school culture has embraced extraversion with open arms. Consider the typical high school, with its slew of social activities and clubs, dances, sporting events, and assemblies.

Introverted students, immersed in this environment, may not approach you with their concerns. Instead, they may work hard to appear more social than is comfortable for them.

The solution is in differentiating for both temperaments.

Extraverts, who tend to be more vocal about their needs and preferences, are easier to differentiate for simply because you're more likely to be aware of what they need. An introverted student may simply go with the flow, choosing the path of least resistance, even if it is uncomfortable for them.

Introverts need an advocate, someone that will support them and help them learn to succeed in an extraverted world.

Integrating a combination of group and individual activities will benefit all of your students. Extraverts, who sometimes struggle with individual work, will learn to become more comfortable working independently. Similarly, introverts will learn those essential skills that group work hones.

Like so many other aspects of education, it is a balancing act. A mindful teacher will be able to structure his class with a combination of independent and team-based work, weaving the two together so that neither the introvert nor the extravert spends too much of their energy on activities that deplete it.

PART II: ADAPTING TO THE INTROVERTED STUDENT

While it is important for all students to step outside of their comfort zones, it is just as important they do not live there.

PREVENTING STUDENT BURNOUT

In high school, I was required to take Spanish, a class in which 30% of the grade was determined by class participation.

The sentiment behind it was valid enough — to properly learn a language, it's important to practice speaking it. For me, though, the idea of speaking out in front of the entire class in a new, foreign language was paralyzing. I didn't even like speaking English in front of others, unless I had time to prepare.

So I didn't.

As a result, the highest grade I was able to receive was a 70%, no matter how well I did on the other activities.

Take a moment to think about the classroom activities you fall back on. Do they involve a lot of group work, socialization, discussion, and debate?

You are probably well-versed in running an extraverted classroom. You may have developed a number of different group-oriented activities, and feel comfortable with stations, jigsaw activities, and group discussions.

These group activities are incredibly important. They teach valuable skills, like teamwork and peer mediation, while allowing the teacher to act as a facilitator, giving students the ability to direct their own learning.

That's the good news.

The bad news?

All of these activities are a recipe for introverted burnout. For many introverts, constant group work is exhausting and overwhelming. Even something as simple as class participation can be intimidating.

As a student, I felt this every day. Constant group work took its toll, and in the case of my Spanish class I chose to lose the participation points rather than agonize over what I was going to say.

Years later, when I was behind the teacher's desk, I was faced with a conundrum.

How did I ensure that all of my students were comfortable, and all of their needs met? I didn't want to unintentionally leave any students in the dust, as my Spanish teacher had.

What I needed was a classroom that was conducive to extraverted social activities, while also creating a stable, structured environment that allowed introverts to feel secure.

I found that the best way to do this was by taking several different factors into consideration: classroom environment, in-class activities, grading systems, and the incorporation of technology.

CLASSROOM ENVIRONMENT

In general, introverts are more susceptible to changes in their environment. They prefer consistency and organization, and they like to know exactly what is expected of them. Loud, bright, constantly active and social classrooms are a sure way to overwhelm your introverted student. On the other hand, extraverts are less fazed by change, and some may even prefer it.

Promoting Productivity in Introverts and Extraverts

Both introverts and extraverts benefit from different environments. When placed in their ideal environments, they thrive. When removed from them, they struggle.

So what does the ideal look like?

While each individual will be different, there are a few general trends that introverts and extraverts tend to gravitate toward.

The Introvert
1. Light, subtle colors
2. Minimal clutter
3. Organized workspace
4. Predictable schedule
5. Soft, ambient sounds or complete silence
6. Limited socialization

The Extravert
1. Bright, invigorating colors
2. Room to spread out
3. A little chaos is manageable
4. Freedom to jump from project to project
5. Inspiring music with a good beat
6. Opportunities to bounce ideas off of others

When setting up your classroom at the beginning of the year, try to find a balance between the ideal environments of both the introvert and the extravert.

Classroom Organization

The classroom can be a messy place. Even the most organized teacher is engaged in an endless battle against paper scraps, dropped pencils, and forgotten assignments.

While the mess can't be avoided all of the time, a clear organizational system will help your introverts and extraverts alike. Your introvert, who craves order and predictability, will benefit from knowing where everything belongs. Your extravert, who may have a natural tendency to spread out a bit, will learn how to remain organized without sacrificing creativity.

This is particularly important if your class involves a lot of group work. Since group activities are already energy consumers for introverted students, adding clutter into the equation will only cause them to burn out more quickly.

To organize your class room effectively, make sure all supplies have a designated, clearly marked home and that the floors are kept clean and clear of trash. Use your students to help in this endeavor!

Classroom Feng Shui

When I was a teacher, my desks moved often. Sometimes they were in a large circle, other times they were arranged in pods or rows. Each arrangement set the tone for the purpose of the class.

This constant movement has the potential to be incredibly overwhelming to introverts, since they are so sensitive to their external environment. When a classroom is inconsistent, it may set them on edge.

Ensure that all of your students are aware of the purpose behind any changes that occur and, if possible, they are told of the changes in advance. When students know ahead of time that, for example, a circle-desk day is a discussion day, they will become less startled and off-balance by the change in their environment.

If your desk arrangement or assigned seats must change frequently, try to incorporate more consistency into the rest of your classroom.

Developing organizational systems, using soothing colors, and designing unchanging nooks and crannies for independent work will help introverted students feel less overwhelmed.

Understandable Expectations

Establishing well-defined, clear expectations and procedures at the beginning of the school year is generally considered good classroom management. It is also an essential element for introvert survival.

Since many introverts perform better in an ordered, predictable environment, they have an automatic desire to know what is expected of them. This includes classroom rules and procedures, as well as the consequences involved.

Setting up these procedures early on and being consistent with them will allow your introverted students to prepare in advance for tasks that otherwise may make them uncomfortable. Seemingly simple tasks, such as turning in work, collecting work missed while absent, or even sharpening a pencil may seem overwhelming if the student does not know the procedure for approaching the situation.

Similarly, by clearly posting important information, such as when assignments are due, your students will be able to prepare effectively. This is particularly important if the assignments have a social component, such as a class presentation or discussion. The use of a class website may also help students plan ahead.

ACTIVITIES

Group work is not going anywhere anytime soon. It's an essential component of a successful classroom, and the skills it teaches are necessary for survival in today's world.

That said, a well-balanced classroom will incorporate both group work and structured, independent activities. Regularly implementing both within the classroom allows introverts and extraverts both to grow outside of their comfort zone.

While your extraverted students may complain that they prefer the more free-form environment that is inherent to group work, it's important to remind them that working individually, or in structured pairs, is also an important skill.

The best way to navigate the opposing needs of introverted and extraverted students is to develop a flow between the two temperaments. Follow group activities with an individual activity, and vice versa. Keep your group activities well-structured, while leaving room for creative expression in individual activities.

Finding this balance is not easy, but it's important, because it will allow all of your students to practice something that does not come naturally to them.

Some of the ideas below detail possible alternatives to group time that will allow introverted students to recharge – both within structured class time and outside of it.

Alternative Recess

Going outside and running amok for half an hour should be every kid's dream, right? Unfortunately, for the introverted child it may be more of a nightmare.

As much as introverts crave structure, they also need time to let their imaginations wander. Introverted students look inward far more often than their extraverted peers, and recess is the perfect time for them to get their creative juices flowing.

By providing students with an alternative to the traditional recess time you're giving them the option of pursuing their true interests. Not every student wants to play tag or fight over the swings. Some would much prefer to stay in the classroom and read, or play in a quieter area with a few select people.

Make sure you set strict boundaries so that students don't abuse this option. See if your school is willing to set aside a place for "quiet recess", like the library or even a certain area of the playground for anyone who wants to play individually or in small, quiet groups. Alternatively, you could establish an indoor recess with a special interest focus, like a book club or a space for drawing.

Independent Activity Time

There are a number of skills that can be learned from independent work. Self-pacing, organization, and personal discipline are just a few benefits of implementing individual work into your class time. The extraverted student learns valuable skills that are not dependent on socialization, while the introverted student has the opportunity to recharge.

Reflections

Incorporating reflection time after a group activity is a great way to buffer in recharge time for your introverts. Not only that, but it allows all of your students to pause and think about the purpose of the activity they just completed.

Pausing for reflection gives students a chance to really analyse the importance of the topic being discussed, as well as its relevance. It's an opportunity for them to tackle higher-level thinking questions independently, and create their own creative solutions. It also provides an avenue through which students can address questions they might have in a non-threatening manner.

Non-Content Based Activities

Setting aside individual time to work on something that is not directly related to your content will give students a bit of a mental break and encourage them to pursue their own interests.

Many schools have implemented silent reading time into their priorities, which is fantastic. It's not just about reading, though. Activities like free writing, card and board games, or computer time are also all great options for the introverted student.

Choice-Based Activities

Student choice is powerful.

When you give a student the chance to choose how they learn, they are taking charge of their own education. As a result, they have a direct stake in what they are learning and tend to take on the responsibility of that choice more readily.

Naturally, when presented with choice, students will choose activities more suited to their temperament. By providing several approaches to the same topic, you naturally differentiate for introverts and extraverts, allowing them to choose the amount of socialization and external stimuli that is appropriate for them.

Student Choice Boards

One of my favorite methods of implementing choice is through student choice boards. Designed to give students controlled freedom over the learning tasks they perform, choice boards are effective throughout the lesson cycle, and they automatically allow for differentiation. They provide a quick and easy way to implement choice in an organized fashion.

Activities within a choice board can include everything from an essay or a skit to a partnered research assignment or a media advertisement. The options are limitless and are adaptable to any grade level or subject area.

There are many, many different types of choice boards. They can be incredibly simple and open-ended, or highly structured. They can be adapted to any subject area and used to access prior knowledge, guide research, or evaluate student understanding.

Structured Group Work

Since group work is not only unavoidable, but critical, creating a structure within groups will help introverts survive. By assigning clear roles within the group, each individual will know what is expected of him or her.

This could be as simple as assigning action roles within the group (leader, recorder, speaker, researcher, etc.). The simple act of providing a set of expectations within the group, rather than allowing it to be free-form, is a relief for many introverts.

Structure within groups also helps to hold students accountable, and a peer-review of their group cooperation can help keep students on task. Groups should never find themselves in a situation where a single student is doing the majority of the work.

One example of structured group work in action is through Edward de Bono's Six Thinking Hats. Using this method, each group member is assigned a different color "thinking hat". Each color represents a slightly different way of approaching the group task.

For example, the student assigned the white hat is responsible for collecting facts, whereas the student assigned the yellow hat focuses on positive outcomes.

This method is adaptable to almost any subject area and grade level, and as soon as a student knows their color they know what is expected of them. For the introvert who craves structure, it is an incredibly useful tool.

For more information about Edward deBono's Six Thinking Hats method, you can visit *www.debonogroup.com*.

Think-Pair-Share

One of the most common structured group activities, the Think-Pair-Share has been around for years. Despite this, it continues to retain its value, incorporating the necessary preparation time many introverts need before feeling comfortable addressing the class.

Additionally, this activity can be adapted to just about any grade level or subject area. The process contains three simple steps:

Think

Assign students something to think about. This could be anything, from word problems to hypothetical scenarios. Have students work on the task independently for a set amount of time.

Pair

Once students have had a chance to work independently, pair them up and give them an opportunity to discuss. This gives introverts, who have had an opportunity to plan their answer, a chance to express it to a single person, which is far less socially stressful than the entire classroom. Similarly, extraverts will be given the opportunity to socialize after a period of silence, which may have been difficult for them.

Share

Finally, allow student pairs to share their final answers with the class, leading to a more detailed discussion of the topic.

By following these steps, the amount of socialization required has been approached in a measured manner that slowly increases. As a result, all of the students become more comfortable discussing the topic at hand.

Independent Study Projects

The ultimate experiment in student choice is the independent study project. And, since most introverts tend to deeply investigate topics of interest, it is well-suited to them. An independent study project will help nurture this natural desire to investigate their interests.

In addition, independent study teaches valuable skills pertaining to research, organization, time management, and presentation. These are skills from which all students, whether introverts or extraverts, can benefit.

Typically, independent study is approached as an extension activity, expanding upon a topic that has already been discussed in detail within the classroom. This is an effective route, though independent study can be sprinkled throughout the lesson cycle, or even the entire year, if approached correctly.

The most important part of an independent project is to incorporate well-defined benchmarks that will allow introverts to prepare themselves, while also keeping extraverts on task and holding all students accountable.

Clear expectations and guidelines are essential here, particularly if projects span a long period of time.

Case Study: The Junior Humanity Project

As an AP Language and Composition instructor, there were certain skills I was required to teach that were well-suited to independent projects. These skills, including analysis, synthesis, and research, were regarded by most students as dry and unimpressive.

To counter this popular opinion, and to provide introverted students an independent outlet, I developed the Junior Humanity Project. With a loose basis on the film Pay it Forward, the concept was simple: students were to choose one aspect of their society that intrigued them, investigate it, propose a change that would improve it, and act on the change.

The project was always assigned at the beginning of the school year, and students were given until April to complete it and submit their findings in a 20-page thesis, the completion of which became somewhat of a rite of passage into senior year.

Throughout the course of the project, my students volunteered with special needs kids, assisted in stem cell research, interviewed social workers, and investigated the moral and legal implications of a variety of civil issues, from arranged marriages to the legalization of recreational drugs.

The benefits of this project were bountiful. Students were able to practice independent research skills, analysis, and synthesis. They achieved the goals of the course, which included argumentation skills and the ability to negotiate and recognize rhetorical strategies used in persuasion.

More importantly, though, each student was given the chance to explore their own interests and make their own mark upon their community. Introverts had the opportunity to dig deep into issues they cared about, while extraverts were able to share their energy and passion with broader audiences through volunteer work and interviews.

RUBRICS

In a perfect world, grades would be a thing of the past. Students would learn based on their intrinsic desire to understand their world, and there would be no arbitrary, numeric system of evaluating their success.

Unfortunately, that perfect world doesn't exist in most schools. With many public schools cracking down on testing and standards, grades are a necessary evil.

With that in mind, clear expectations go a long way. When it comes to performing well in school, introverted students are often more successful when they know exactly how their work will be graded.

Because introverts like to mentally prepare themselves, it benefits them to understand grading expectations ahead of time — particularly with larger, more demanding assignments like essays, projects, or presentations. The easiest way to accomplish this is by creating a structured rubric, clearly outlining the parameters of an assignment and how it will be graded.

These rubrics are not just helpful for your introverts. Extraverted students will be presented with a roadmap to follow as well, and you as the teacher will find grading far more streamlined when you have a rubric.

Guidelines for Rubrics

Rubrics come in all shapes and sizes, and many of them can be found on teacher exchange sites online.

If you're developing your own rubrics from scratch, though, there are a few things to keep in mind:

1)   *Begin with the end in mind*
      Ask yourself what you want your students to accomplish. What does the ideal completed project look like, and is it

realistic for your students?

2) ***Assign a clear point value***
The largest benefit of rubrics is that students learn where their points are coming from. Whether it's a holistic scoring process or a 100-point assignment, it's important that students understand where your numbers are coming from.

3) ***Specifically state student expectations***
In addition to stating a point value, make sure that students understand exactly what will allow them to earn the maximum possible points. Give a brief explanation of your expectations.

4) ***Leave space for creativity and flexibility***
Don't be so rigid that student creativity is stifled. Allow for some interpretation in the verbiage. Being too rigid will isolate your extraverts and even some introverts may begin to think that your assignments are dry.

Designing Your Rubric

There are many different resources for rubric design. When I was teaching, Rubistar.com was my go-to platform for quick, customized rubrics.

I also frequently developed my own, custom rubrics right within a Microsoft Word document. Once I set up an initial template, it became easy to swap out the content and point values for different assignments.

On the next page is a simple sample rubric example that were created in a Microsoft Word Document. It was created for a primary school classroom that is studying the different states in the U.S.

What's Your State?
Project Rubric

_____ / 20   **State Overview**
Poster includes an image of the state, the state slogan, and the year it became part of The United States of America

_____ / 20   **State Facts**
Images representing 5 interesting facts about the state are on the poster. For example: State fossil, state bird, U.S. presidents born within the state, famous historical events, etc.

_____ / 10   **My State is Known For**
What makes your state famous? What does everyone know it for? Depict at least three claims to fame on the poster.

_____ / 50   **Presentation**
Teach the class about your new state. Tell them all about why the class should go on a field trip to that state and what makes it unique. Use your poster as a guide.

_____ / 100 Total

Teacher Notes:

In addition to the structured rubric, there is also a section for teacher notes. This gives the instructor an opportunity for qualitative feedback as well as quantitative feedback.

In and of itself, this is a rather simplistic rubric. It provides general guidelines while allowing room for creative expression. Students are not being told what their final product should look like, but rather the elements that should be incorporated into it.

Certain activities and subjects may call for more in-depth rubrics. No matter how detailed your rubric is, the primary advantages here are that they create structure for the introvert while removing subjectivity from grading. They also create a situation where the teacher is not forced to reinvent the wheel each time an assignment is created. Just remember not to be overly structured – otherwise your more free-form students may suffer.

The Class Rubric

Rubric creation itself can be an activity. When going over a new assignment with your class, give them an opportunity to decide what should be expected of them.

Similar to the choice board assignments mentioned earlier, the rubric creation process gives students more say over their educational experience. It forces the students into the role of the teacher, helping them determine what a quality finished project should look like. As a result, your students are likely to feel more invested in the assignment.

Interestingly enough, I've found that students tend to grade themselves far more strictly than their teachers, particularly when the students themselves play an active role in the formation of the assignment and its expectations.

TECHNOLOGY

The modern classroom is a tech savvy classroom, and this suits the introverted student just fine. Technology offers an unprecedented opportunity, putting social control back in the hands of the individual. By taking advantage of technology, you can give your introverted students the chance to find their voice.

Creating a Safe Digital Space

As the instructor, it is incredibly important to facilitate any online discussions. Cyber bullying is a very real problem, and it's important to remain a steady presence in any digital activities. Online assignments should be an extension of the classroom, and as such, class rules should apply.

Online Collaboration Platforms

The internet may be the single most beneficial invention for introverts. It simultaneously makes socialization possible for anyone, at any time, while removing the most stressful and exhausting component: face-to-face interaction. A student using the internet to communicate is able to decide exactly how much they want to participate, and in what capacity.

Collaboration platforms like Google Drive and Prezi are free and allow students to interact and collaborate without the added pressure of in-person socialization. Groups are able to work in the classroom or remotely, without having to organize schedules or decide on a meeting place.

Online Discussion

Class participation is often a contributing factor in a student's grade, which can be incredibly stressful for an introvert. Since their extraverted peers are more likely to speak up quickly, introverts are often drowned out. As discussed earlier, introverts often take more time to formulate an answer that they are comfortable sharing, and by the time they are ready to participate the discussion may have moved on.

By incorporating an online component to class discussions, this problem can be alleviated. Instead of declaring a conversation complete at the end of a class, allow students to make follow-up points and counterpoints digitally. Students could participate in an online forum, or they could simply e-mail their responses.

Digital Presentations and Projects

The rise of social media is incredibly useful for class activities. There are endless opportunities to incorporate platforms like Pinterest, Twitter, and Facebook into the classroom. More formalized digital projects, such as blogs, are already popular in many classrooms.

For example, instead of creating and presenting a physical poster or presentation, students could create a Pinterest board to represent their understanding of a concept. Instead of presenting it in front of the class, they can share the board with their classmates and submit a blog post that explains the purpose of each pin.

Both Instagram and Twitter rely heavily on hashtags. By assigning a class or project hashtag, students can send out tweets and images that relate to concepts being studied. There are tools such as Hashtagify.me that you can use to see if a hashtag is already being used or not.

Apps and Gaming Platforms

For some reason, video games seem to have a bad reputation. They're often seen as frivolous and mind numbing, rather than enlightening and engaging. This is unfortunate, because apps and video games can provide amazing supplements to class content.

There are literally hundreds of apps that students can download to their tablet or smartphone to help them learn about different concepts, from math to science to SAT prep.

Incorporating digital games and apps into your class gives all of your students an outlet that is both educational and fun. Providing incentives, like bonus points for completing certain levels, can up the ante and get students engaged in a way that is not overwhelmingly social.

Virtual Nooks and Crannies

Sometimes your control over class environment is limited. You may share a classroom, or there may be rules regarding what you are allowed to bring into your class.

For example, one year I had group tables rather than desks. Students were forced to sit in groups every day, even when group work was not being completed. This was the only arrangement I had available at the time, and it was not particularly helpful for the introverts in my classroom.

My solution was to create virtual walls. The easiest way to do this is by allowing students the option of putting headphones on as they complete individual tasks.

Students can choose to listen to the music that is most helpful to their concentration. The sound of the music becomes white noise that blocks out the rest of the activity around the student. Alternatively, if students prefer complete silence, they can put ear plugs in.

Background Noise and Performance

Have you ever noticed that some people insist on listening to music while they work, while others prefer complete silence? Studies have shown that while extraverts are proficient at working in a variety of environments, introvert performance suffers when music and other noise is introduced into the environment (Dobbs, 2011).

Of course, doing this requires clearly structured rules. Students must be willing to remove their headphones or ear plugs when you need their attention, and their music should not be turned up so loud that the entire class can hear it.

This is often a better option than playing your own music over speakers, because it allows students to choose what they want to listen to and it provides a sense of isolation when needed.

Since introverts tend to be distracted easily by external stimuli, this can be a great way to help them focus on their assignment.

FINAL THOUGHTS

While this section relies heavily on introverted accommodations, it is important to remember the need for balance. Exchanging group work for individualized activities all of the time will only result in the isolation of your extraverted students. The goal is to include everyone.

Remember your own temperament, and be wary of leaning too far towards what makes you comfortable. It's easy to fall into the habit of assigning the sort of work that you would enjoy if you were a student, and it's difficult sometimes to put yourself in the shoes of those who learn and interact differently from you.

Developing a class culture that embraces extraversion and introversion will allow each to learn valuable skills from the other.

PART III: SELF-CARE FOR THE INTROVERTED TEACHER

"Self-care is not about self-indulgence. It's about self-preservation." – Audrey Lorde

RECOGNIZING TEACHER BURNOUT

When I first started teaching high school my class sizes averaged around 35 students. Sometimes they would climb as high as 45 students, with the number of bodies outpacing the number of desks I had available.

With eight classes cycling through my room each day, my total student count became absurdly high. One year, I topped out at around 250 students, an exhausting number of sixteen-year-olds to coerce into paying attention to an English class.

Every day I would return home with a massive headache and the desire to lock myself in my bedroom. My friendships, relationships, and teaching suffered as I dug my heels in, resisting the very idea of returning to the crowded, noisy school that felt more like a prison every single day.

Teaching: A Highly Social Career

Students, teachers, administrators, and parents all vie for attention, and sometimes they can be incredibly demanding. There is very little opportunity within a typical school day for alone time. Often, even conference periods and lunch hours are taken up by various responsibilities.

In Part I, we looked at the various symptoms of student burnout. Those same afflictions can be signs of an overwhelmed teacher. Symptoms such as headaches and fatigue, along with irritability and a lack of interest are common signs of an impending burnout.

Whether you are an introvert or an extravert, you are probably familiar with the feeling of being completely overwhelmed. Teacher burnout is in no way a strictly introverted phenomenon; however, introverted teachers may be more susceptible.

Despite these challenges, there are many phenomenal introverted teachers.

Fighting an Uphill Battle

As an introverted teacher myself, I felt as though I was constantly on the brink of burnout.

It was unfortunate, because I loved teaching. The actual act of passing along knowledge to my students, facilitating their discovery, and watching as they grasped new concepts delighted me.

I lived for those moments when my students found themselves actually enjoying the intricacies of rhetoric.

Even so, I was exhausted. Eventually, I became too exhausted to enjoy even those moments of success.

I realized that I needed to adopt strategies that would help me recover faster, or avoid social burnout altogether. I needed to teach in a way that did not compromise my own health and sanity.

At the time, I didn't fully understand my introversion; I simply knew that I was burned out. I didn't know why. What I did know was that something needed to change.

If you're an educator, you're likely spending vast quantities of your energy currency every day. If you're an introverted teacher, you can deplete your energy reserves very quickly. Once you're on the brink of a breakdown, it can seem impossible to catch up and find the time to recharge.

Because of the ever-demanding requirements of the field, and because burnout is almost always looming on the horizon, it's essential to take preventative action.

The more you do to prepare yourself, the better off you'll be when you start to feel overwhelmed.

PREVENTATIVE CARE & RECOVERY

Burnout is not just an annoying side effect of a demanding job, and if taken lightly it can be debilitating.

Introverts facing continuous overstimulation and burnout can experience seriously detrimental effects on their health and relationships. Just like when you overdraft your bank account and face penalty charges, there are penalties for over-drafting your energy account.

As a teacher, you want to be the best that you can be for your students. You also want to be able to enjoy your personal interests and relationships without feeling as though maintaining them is an extra burden. It's hard to maintain a positive and professional attitude when you're constantly at the end of your rope.

There are ways to recover from burnout when it strikes, but it is even more valuable to prevent it from happening altogether. Incorporating preventative self-care into your routine can go a long way when you're deep in the throes of the school year.

Follow these tips to help make your school year smoother, healthier, and happier.

Define Your Point Zero
Point Zero is the furthest place from burnout. It is your ideal environment, full of what you would do if all of your social responsibilities magically fell away. It may be a physical place (and we'll talk about how to create one), or it may be a simple state of mind.

Defining your Point Zero can be a little tricky. There's a tendency to assume that it is the polar opposite of what is causing you burnout, but that may not always be the case.

When I was teaching, I initially thought that my Point Zero was a quiet place where I could just sit and do absolutely nothing, while talking to absolutely no one. Instead of opinionated colleagues, demanding students, and a finicky administration, I was free to relax and be utterly unproductive.

Inevitably, when summer vacation arrived, I would immediately try to fulfill this fantasy. I would lock myself away and shut out the world.

Unfortunately, I quickly learned that this wasn't actually what I wanted. I became restless and bored. I would find projects, start them, and then abandon them. I would dwell on the upcoming year, and then berate myself for not enjoying my break – after all, this is what I wanted, right?

Except that it wasn't.

I thought my Point Zero was simply the opposite of what was stressing me out – doing nothing instead of doing everything. I was wrong. I was just as miserable doing nothing, only in a different way.

Through some trial and error, I've discovered that my Point Zero isn't about doing nothing and being stress-free. My Point Zero involves self-driven projects that are deadline-driven and completed largely by myself or with one other person. It involves the ability to move between my projects and my hobbies with ease, and keeping in close touch with one or two friends who are willing to communicate primarily over the computer rather than by phone or face-to-face.

Finding your own Point Zero is important, but it isn't always easy, especially if you are riding the edge of a burnout. However, there are a few steps you can take to try and identify your Point Zero.

Paint the big picture

You can't build a house without planning its layout. Similarly, you can't establish your Point Zero without understanding how you want it to look and feel.

Do you want your Point Zero to encourage relaxation or productivity? Is it a place for specific projects or hobbies? Is it dark or bright? Does it contain mindless distractions or focused, mindful activities?

The answer will be different for everyone. What is important is that your Point Zero allows you to earn back energy, rather than spend more of it.

If you're not sure where to start, take a look at the questionnaire below. Take a few minutes to answer each of the questions honestly.

Defining your Point Zero: Questionnaire

If you took the day off of work and had no other responsibilities, what would you spend your day doing?

If you took the week off of work and had no other responsibilities, what would you spend the week doing?

If you took an entire year off of work, and had no other responsibilities, what would you want to spend that year doing? Assume that you have unlimited funds.

How often do you want to interact with other people face-to-face? How many people, ideally, would you interact with at a time?

What sort of hobbies, projects, or activities make you feel fulfilled?

How many times a week would you like to go out with a large group of people? How many times a month?

Find Your Stressors

Of course, the other side of the coin is to think about what you don't want.

Take a few minutes and think about what exhausts you in your day-to-day routine. Think about when you've been overwhelmed recently — particularly if this is "normal" (that is, not caused by some dramatic life change such as a death in the family, being laid off, etc.). What factors were present?

Use the questions below to help you identify your stressors.

Finding your Stressors: Questionnaire

What physical places do you try to avoid, if possible? For example: The school hallways, cafeteria, the grocery store, the bank, etc.

What characteristics do those places share? For example: open/closed, light/dark, crowded, noisy, etc.

Are there any specific people who contribute to your sense of being overwhelmed? What specifically about them is overstimulating?

What situations do you dread? Think of places or events you try to skip out on, or leave early from.

Don't think too hard about your answers. Just go with the first thing that comes to mind. And don't worry — just because certain people may overwhelm you at times, that doesn't mean you need to abandon your friends. It simply means that you may need to approach your friendship a little differently.

Getting to Point Zero is about finding what makes you happy naturally. Then, once you've found that, you can slowly add other elements (like that slightly high-energy friend) back into your life in a manageable way.

Once you know what your Point Zero is, the next step is to make it accessible.

Build Your Sanctuary

The easiest way to earn back your spent energy currency is by creating a sanctuary that will allow you to return to Point Zero quickly. Doing this will allow you to step away from stressors and block out the social noise that may be hurting you.

Your Physical Sanctuary

As a teacher, you may not have much control over your space. What control you do have should be exercised with attention to yourself as well as your students.

My second year teaching I created a reading nook in my classroom. No one batted an eye as I hauled in my extra couch, rolled out a carpet, and shelved box upon box of books. I was an English teacher, so the homey little corner, adorned with Harry Potter posters and inspirational quotes, made perfect sense.

Want to know a secret?

I didn't build that nook for my students.

Most of the time, my students were too busy to use it. I built that reading nook for myself, so that I had a nearby place I could retreat to when my energy levels were low.

Even though I am no longer in the classroom, I still take time to create a personal sanctuary. There are a few key factors that go into this space:

1. *Organization*
    I try to make sure my workspace is clear of everything but my laptop and perhaps a notebook and pen. As soon as clutter starts working its way onto my desk, it destroys the sanctuary.

2. *Natural Elements*
    My desk faces the window and receives a lot of natural light. I'm a huge fan of the outdoors, and if I can't be actively wandering around in the woods I want to recreate as much of that as possible. If it's not too hot or cold I'll open the windows as well.

    When I was in the classroom, I didn't have a window. Instead, I surrounded myself with pictures of nature, potted plants, and colors that reminded me of the outdoors.

3. *Snacks*
    I usually make myself a cup of coffee or tea and a small snack before settling in. I feel calmer while working than simply sitting and relaxing, and I want to make sure that I have enough fuel to keep me going.

Your own sanctuary needs to be structured in a way that suits your needs. It should offer consistency and stability, and be a place of recovery, rest, and reflection — a place where you can work on what is important to you.

Your sanctuary can be anywhere. It can be a bedroom, a meditation room, a corner of your classroom, or a nearby park. The size and shape of the place doesn't matter as much as the nature and purpose of it.

Introverts are sensitive to changes in their environment. This includes temperature changes, noise levels, colors, and the general atmosphere of a room. All of these different components should be taken into account when creating a physical sanctuary.

To start creating sanctuary, look back at the Point Zero that you created for yourself. You want to develop as much of a physical manifestation of that as possible.

In general, there are some physical factors that introvert-friendly sanctuaries will share:

1. *Privacy*

   Remember, being around external stimulation is one of the most draining parts of an introvert's life. This is a particularly prevalent problem with teachers. Even if it's just a corner of the room, designating a "don't bother me" zone can do wonders.

   During the school day you may not be able to tell your students to simply leave you alone. Try to find time during passing period, lunch, or before or after school to use your sanctuary. Even if it's just for five minutes, you'll be surprised how much it helps.

2. *Quiet*

   Conversations, loud music, television, and anything else that can't be considered "white noise" is sure to disrupt your sanctuary. If you're a music person, look for quiet, ambient sounds that set a relaxing mood. Otherwise, try to ensure that your sanctuary is as silent as possible.

3. *Color-Conscious*

   There are entire books about the psychology of color – usually marketing books. Ever wonder why McDonald's is red and yellow? It's all because of the secret language of color. Different colors make us think and feel differently. For example, red provides a sense of urgency, whereas blue is more calming.

   When it comes to your sanctuary, figure out which color combinations settle your mind. For me, this tends to be a lot of blues and greens, and I surround myself with them.

4. *Focused*

   Whatever your purpose is in visiting your sanctuary, it should be clear, and getting started should be simple.

   If you want to use it as a place to read, make sure there are plenty of books nearby. If you're planning on meditating, opt for comfy cushions. If it's a place to work, have your laptop, notepad, and other essentials on hand. Clear your mind and remember to breathe.

Your Mental Sanctuary

Unfortunately, a physical sanctuary is not always an option. Even if you are able to create one for yourself, burnout may strike at a time when it's inaccessible – in the middle of a class, during a meeting, or at a party, for instance.

If this happens, it's time to take a mental vacation. Just five minutes of separation from what is overstimulating can make a massive difference. Create a strategy that allows you to refocus on what's important.

Here's the strategy that works for me:

1. *Excuse yourself and find a quiet place.*

    My default hideout is the bathroom, so long as there isn't a long line. No one will bother you if you're locked in a bathroom stall for a few minutes. Even if you're teaching, you can usually find someone to cover your class for just a few minutes. Your car is another great alternative.

2. *Close your eyes and take a few deep, full breaths.*

    Make sure you completely fill your lungs, so that your entire stomach expands. Count to five as you inhale, hold the breath for another count of five, then slowly exhale for a count of ten. Repeat this process until you start to feel more centered.

    There is a lot of value in deep breathing exercises. When we get overwhelmed, we often forget to take deep enough breaths, and as a result we are getting less oxygen. This only works against you, adding to the sense of overstimulation. These deep breaths will get oxygen flowing again, and kick in the body's natural relaxation rhythm.

3. *Remind yourself why what you are doing is valuable.*

    Take a moment to think about what is stressing you out and why it's important to follow through.

Try and complete the simple statement below.

Fill in the Blanks

"I am doing this because _____, and it is worth my valuable time and energy because _____."

For example:

> "I am incorporating this group activity into my classroom because it is helping my students understand an important concept. This is worth my valuable time and energy because I want my students to learn to work well together as a team."

If you can't find any immediate value in what you're doing that's alright. Sometimes we are forced into situations that seem pointless. If this happens, take a few moments to simply visualize your physical sanctuary while you breathe.

4. *Think only as far ahead as the next half hour.*
   Set a success goal for yourself. It could be to strike up a conversation with someone, to offer a lesson suggestion, or to interact positively with one of your more difficult students. Make sure your goal is actionable and achievable.

5. *Repeat as necessary.*
   Check on yourself again in half an hour. Have you met your goal? Whether you have or not, be kind to yourself and duck away for another quick break if necessary.

The particulars of this process may be different for everyone, but the basic premise of removing yourself from the situation for just five minutes is important. It is impossible to ward off over-stimulation by remaining in a stimulating environment.

Combining both the use of your physical and your mental sanctuary, even just once a day, can go a long way towards warding off the burnout that introverted teachers begin to feel very early in the school year.

AVOIDING UNNECESSARY COMMITMENT

Over-commitment and teaching go hand-in-hand. There are endless committees, clubs, activities, and duties that you can add to your plate — on top of your usual day-to-day work. While you may legitimately enjoy some of these commitments, it's important not to over-commit yourself.

One of the unfortunate battles that an introvert faces is finding equilibrium in a world that is designed for the extravert. The best defense that the introvert can have is learning when to say "no".

As an introvert, you have to be careful before committing yourself beyond what is required of you. Certain commitments may be worth your time, but you should balance the energy you will be spending against the amount of recovery time it will allow you.

When faced with the option of taking on new commitments, consider the following:

1. *Is this something I am passionate about?*
   The more a commitment gets you fired up, the longer you can avoid burnout.

   If you're truly passionate about fundraising, then it may be worth your time to help students raise money for new band equipment.

   If you love science, chaperoning a trip to the local museum could be a great option. Getting to know students outside of the day-to-day of the classroom can build a great mutual support system.

2. *How will participating benefit me and/or my students?*
   What is the gain in sacrificing your time and energy? Is it

worth the trade-off?

3. *How much time will this require?*
   Always assume that a commitment will take more time than you initially think.

   For example, my creative writing club used to host release parties whenever a movie was released that adapted a popular book (like *Harry Potter*). The event itself was only a few hours, but it took several weeks, and many after-school meetings, to prepare.

4. *How much social stimulation will this require?*
   Assisting in the school book drive requires a very different type of socialization than helping to chaperone the weekend football game.

   Consider the amount of stimulation you will be presented with if you agree to the commitment, and decide whether it is acceptable.

5. *How many other commitments do I currently have?*
   It can be easy to get into the habit of always saying "yes," but before you know it you're up to your eyeballs in activities and events.

   Before you agree to something new, think about what you've already agreed to. How much time have you already given, and how much more are you willing to donate? How much of your time outside of school hours will you need to commit?

6. *Will I be able to find time to recharge once I've completed the commitment?*
   If you are going straight from one commitment to another, on top of your time teaching, and it is keeping

you after school well into the evening every night with no end in sight, it may be too much.

Make sure you build in time to recharge, and remember to ask for help when things become hard to handle on your own

Rather than committing to many different activities, try finding one that you are passionate about. Use it as a way to remain involved without stretching yourself too thin.

Identify your stressors, and if a commitment contains too many of them it may be best to pass.

ORGANIZING YOUR LIFE

Many introverts are also planners. They like to mentally prepare for the road ahead. This is why surprising an introvert isn't always a good idea, especially if it interferes with the mental plan they've already set for the day.

That said, organization doesn't *always* come naturally — even to those who may benefit from it most. All through college and my first few years teaching I threw organization to the wind, simply tackling problems as they arose. It was exhausting and stressful, but I felt as though I didn't have the time to develop a system that would help me.

Eventually, enough was enough and I started to set up processes that would help me remain organized and focused. It was a huge help, and the amount of stress that it's saved me has been immeasurable.

Organization skills are beneficial to introverts and extraverts alike, and an organized environment can help introverts ward off burnout.

Organized Calendar

Keeping an organized record of important dates and times will help you mentally prepare for what is coming. Whether this is a paper calendar or a digital one, the more organized it is the better.

In my case, I use Google's calendar feature. It is color coordinated between my various activities (work, personal, family, travel, bills, etc.) and syncs between my computer and my phone. This makes it easy to stay organized while on the go.

Task Lists

A to-do list for your day is an incredibly simple way to incorporate more order into your life. By keeping an account of what you want to accomplish within a day, you are able to hold yourself accountable.

As with calendars, this can be accomplished both online and offline. My favorite online platform for creating task lists is Trello, which has an incredibly robust interface.

More often than not, though, I write my lists by hand. Writing to-do lists isn't difficult, but there are a few strategies I tend to implement to encourage productivity.

Write your list first thing in the morning

Or, even more effectively, the day before when the list of items you didn't complete that day is fresh on your mind. But don't start anything until your list is written. Don't open your computer, don't check your e-mail. Sit and write your list. Brain dump everything you need to do for the day.

Cut out the fat

Do you absolutely have to do everything on your list today? Be honest with yourself.

If there are things that could potentially wait, and your list is becoming a bit too long for comfort, start slicing and dicing. Cut out what isn't essential, or move it to a secondary "if there's time" list.

Intersperse simple tasks with more difficult tasks

Once you have your final list of items, start organizing. If you can help it, split up your difficult tasks, putting an easier task in between each one. This will give your brain a bit of a break.
It may also be worth starting your day with the most difficult task on your list, to get it over with and behind you.

Include a few fun items

Even if it's silly, it's nice to have something to look forward to. One of the items on my to-do list while teaching was frequently something along the lines of, "Reward yourself with a Frappuccino!"

I always looked forward to the moment when I reached that item on my list and was able to pull into the nearest coffee shop. If you don't have time to leave campus, keep snacks on hand or take a mental break to watch some cute cat videos on the Internet.

Time yourself

When working through a task list, it can be easy to get caught up in a single item. Unfortunately, spending hours upon hours on a single task with no breaks can be counter-productive. Instead, schedule in small breaks that allow you time to mentally recharge.

Structured Breaks

Particularly when working in a socially demanding environment, it's important to make sure that you schedule some breaks into your day. This goes back to creating a sanctuary for yourself. Block out time where you retreat, recollect, and reenergize.

If this isn't possible, at least take a few quick mental breaks by trying the breathing exercise detailed in the previous chapter.

The value of a brain break

You may already incorporate brain breaks into your classroom activities, but have you made them a priority in your life? Studies have shown that giving your mind a few minutes of downtime can really help you re-establish your focus – whether you're an introvert or an extravert.

Some of the best brain breaks involve leaving your work behind altogether. Physical exercise, like walking or light yoga, can help you refocus, and a change in environment can spark new ideas.

I'm a big fan of the Pomodoro method. It's a simple series of 25 minute spurts of work, followed by either short 5 minute breaks or longer 15 minute breaks. By working in bursts of 25 minutes at a time, I'm infinitely more productive overall. You can find free Pomodoro timers online (give tomato-timer.com a try).

Meditation is another alternative that can be incredibly helpful. There are fantastic guided meditation resources available online.

My favorite is Headspace, which leads you on ten-minute guided sessions that are designed to refocus your mind and return you to equilibrium. Using this app, you can meditate on the fly, no physical sanctuary required. There are also thousands of free meditation videos available online through YouTube and other channels.

FINAL THOUGHTS

Today's school climate is one of noise, crowds, and constant stimulation. This can be hard on the introverted student and teacher alike, but it isn't completely unmanageable. Incorporating a few simple changes into your day-to-day routine can go a long way.

These strategies don't stop at the classroom door, either. For many teachers, their sense of burnout is only compounded by the fact that they go home to a busy, hectic family life.

Taking these same strategies and applying them to your entire day, not just your work day, can help you enjoy a more productive, fulfilled life overall.

PART IV: NEXT STEPS

"In a gentle way, you can shake the world." – Mahatma Gandhi

AN EVOLVING DIALOGUE

Join the Conversation

As our understanding of personality and temperament changes, and as classroom pedagogy evolves, the way in which introverts and extraverts interact and learn is also changing. There is an urgent need for a continuous, open dialogue between both introverts and extraverts.

The Adaptive Introvert is a community where you can join this dialogue. It is a place where you can find a community dedicated to helping introverted students and teachers succeed.

Through this forum, teachers, administrators, and others are able to contribute their own thoughts and resources to this discussion. I'd like to invite you to join the conversation and share your own story.

To gain access to this group, simply visit us online at *adaptiveintrovert.com* and click on "Join the Community."

The Adaptive Introvert exists as a platform for collaboration and positive growth for all students, educators, extraverts, and introverts alike. Our end goal is to create a positive environment for our students and ourselves.

I look forward to sharing stories, advice, and tips that will help both the introvert and the extravert thrive in today's educational climate. Please feel free to contact me with any questions or comments regarding this book.

Best,

Jessi Honard, M.Ed

RESOURCES AND SUGGESTED READING

Burruss, J., & Kaenzig, L. (1991). Introversion: The Often Forgotten Factor Impacting the Gifted. Virginia Association for the Gifted Newsletter, Fall(21).

Byrd, I. (n.d.). Make Your Class Cozy For Gifted Introverts. Retrieved May 27, 2015, from http://www.byrdseed.com/make-your-class-cozy-for-gifted-introverts/

Cain, S. (2012). Quiet: The power of introverts in a world that can't stop talking. New York: Crown.

Dobbs, S.A. (2011). The effect of background music and noise on the cognitive test performance of introverts and extraverts. Applied Cognitive Psychology, 25(2), 307-313.

Eckstut, J., & Eckstut, A. (2013). Secret Language of Color: Science, Nature, History, Culture, Beauty of Red, Orange, Yellow, Green, Blue, & Violet First Edition Edition. Retrieved August 19, 2015 from http://www.amazon.com/Secret-Language-Color-Science-History/dp/1579129498

Free personality test | 16Personalities. (n.d.). Retrieved June 21, 2015, from http://www.16personalities.com/free-personality-test

Henjum, A. (1982). Introversion: A misunderstood "individual difference" among students. Education, 103(1), 39.

Laney, M. (2005). The hidden gifts of the introverted child: Helping your child thrive in an extroverted world. New York: Workman Pub.

Puddicombe, Andy. (n.d.). Get some Headspace. Retrieved July 29, 2015 from http://www.headspace.com

RubiStar Home. (n.d.). Retrieved June 21, 2015, from http://rubistar.4teachers.org/index.php

Six Thinking Hats. (n.d.). Retrieved July 29, 2015 from
http://www.debonogroup.com/six_thinking_hats.php

Ugur, S. (2004). A Synthesis of Research on Psychological Types of Gifted
Adolescents. The Journal of Secondary Gifted Education, XV(2), 70-
79.

ABOUT THE AUTHOR

Jessica Honard is a writer, educator, and speaker. Originally from Cleveland, Ohio, she earned her degree in English from The Ohio State University. From there, she packed her bags spent the next five years teaching high school English in Houston, Texas. While there she also earned her M.Ed. from Lamar University.

Since leaving the classroom, Jessica has focused on remaining connected with the education community. She has done this through the development of curriculum and the presentation of professional development workshops. In 2015, she created The Adaptive Introvert, an online community through which introverted educators can share their experiences and advice.

These days, Jessica lives in California where she works as a full-time writer and speaker.

CPSIA information can be obtained
at www.ICGtesting.com
Printed in the USA
LVOW04s0038060516
486873LV00022B/559/P